The Complete

Slow Cooker
Cookbook 2022

The Complete
Slow Cooker
Cookbook 2022

<u>From Appetizers to Desserts</u>

 Days Easy Recipes for Delicious & Healthy Crock Pot Homemade Meals

By Kristy Torley

Copyright © 2021 by Kristy Torley

All rights reserved.
No part of this book may be reproduced in any form or by any electronic or mechanical means, including information storage and retrieval systems, without written permission from the author, except for the use of brief quotations in a book review.

CONTENTS

Introduction 1

PART 1:
Chapter One: The Basics Of Slow Cooking 3
Chapter Two: A Guide To Slow Cooking 4

PART 2: *RECIPES* *5*
Chapter Three: Easy Appetizers 5
    Spinach Artichoke Dip 6
    Bean Dip 7
    Boiled Peanuts 8
    Bacon Stuffed Mushrooms 9
    Little Smokies 10
Chapter Four: Beef, Pork, And Lamb *11*
    Beef Bourguignon 12
    Beef And Broccoli 13
    Mississippi Roast 14
    Beef And Barley Soup 15
    Pork Loin Roast 16
    Pork Casserole 17
    Texas Pulled Pork 18
    Garlic Balsamic Pork Loin 19
    Slow Cooked Pork Chops 20
    Brown Sugar Glazed Ham 21
    Slow Cooker Lamb Shoulder 22
    Lamb With Olives And Potatoes 23
Chapter Five: Poultry 24
    Honey Garlic Chicken 25
    Herbed Slow-Cooker Chicken 26
    Chicken And Potatoes 27
    Slow Cooker Chicken With Garlic 28
    Slow Cooker Chicken Chili 29

Chapter Six: Seafood ... 30
- Seafood Cioppino ... 31
- Slow Cooker Seafood Stew ... 32
- Shrimp Scampi ... 33
- Shrimp Boil ... 34
- Sausage And Shrimp Gumbo ... 35

Chapter Seven: Vegetables, Grains And Legumes ... 36
- Slow Cooker Aubergines ... 37
- Slow Cooker Ratatouille ... 38
- Aubergine And Chickpea Stew ... 39
- Mushrooms With Ricotta And Pesto ... 40
- Sweet Potato And Coconut Curry ... 41
- Spiced Carrot And Lentil Soup ... 42
- Slow Cooker Beans ... 43
- Slow Cooker Masala Lentils ... 44
- Mediterranean Bulgur And Lentils ... 45
- Vegetable Bean Soup ... 46
- Bean And Barley Stew ... 47
- Bean Soup With Sweet Potatoes ... 48

Chapter Eight: Stocks, Sides And Sauces ... 49
- Slow Cooker Chicken Stock ... 50
- Slow cooker Bone Broth ... 51
- Slow Cooker Spaghetti Sauce ... 52
- Slow Cooker Tomato Sauce ... 53
- Caramelized Onions ... 54
- Spiced Applesauce ... 55

Chapter Nine: Dessert ... 56
- Chocolate Caramel Cake ... 57
- Blackberry Cobbler ... 58
- Peanut Butter Chocolate Chip Blondies ... 59
- S'mores Cake ... 60
- Peach Cobbler ... 61

CONCLUSION 62

INTRODUCTION

Do you have an electric slow cooker that you want to put to better use? Do you want some recipes that require minimal supervision and your active kitchen time? Well, here is a perfect read for you! Now you can cook a variety of poultry meals, beef, lamb, pork, vegetables, grain and desserts in your slow cooker using the recipe collection shared in this book. You have to admit that slow-cooked food has a distinct flavour that no other cuisine can match. Traditional slow cooking had a number of drawbacks, including the need for regular supervision, which was one of the primary reasons why most people abandoned slow cooking. Slow cooking has never been easier than it is now, thanks to the introduction of electric slow cookers. All you have to do now to cook in an electric slow cooker is set the time and temperature, then leave the food in the cooker, covered, and the machine will do the rest. The cooking temperature is kept low by the digitally regulated heating system, which protects the food from burning.

PART 1:

CHAPTER ONE:
THE BASICS OF SLOW COOKING

Slow cookers prepare meals at a low temperature for 4 to 8 hours. The nutrients in the meal remain in the food because of the lower temperature. Any nutrients lost in the liquid due to heat are simply reabsorbed into the food being in a sealed unit, whether using an electric slow cooker or a casserole dish in the oven. Cooking for longer periods of time enhances flavour and eliminates the need for additional seasoning or sauces. Spices and herbs, on the other hand, provide richness by imparting their goodness and aroma to the food.

Benefits of Slow Cooking

While the slow cooker isn't ideal for every cooking method, it does provide a number of major benefits by offering an effortless slow cooking experience. If you are planning to buy a slow cooker, keep reading to learn about some of the advantages of slow cooking.

- The lower cooking temperatures reduce the risk of burning the food items that tend to stick to the bottom of a pan or burn in an oven.
- Tough cheap meats, such as chuck steaks, roast, and less-lean stewing cattle, are tenderized by the long slow cooking.
- For many venison meals, the slow cooker is an ideal choice. The slow cooker keeps your oven and stovetop free for other cooking, and it's an excellent choice for large parties or holiday meals.
- Scrubbing many pots and pans is unnecessary. Most of the time, you'll only have to clean the slow cooker and a few prep items.
- Slow cookers consume less energy than conventional electric ovens.
- Unlike a huge oven, the slow cooker does not heat up the kitchen, which is a big bonus on a hot summer day.
- A slow cooker is easy to transport. It can be taken from the kitchen to the office or to a party. Simply plug it in and eat.
- A slow cooker can be easily left unattended all day. Before going to work, you can put the ingredients for a recipe in it and come home to supper. Whether you work from home or not, a slow cooker meal is a wonderful alternative for a hectic day.

CHAPTER TWO:
A GUIDE TO SLOW COOKING

Slow cookers are particularly advantageous for individuals who do not have enough time to prepare lunch. You may put all of the ingredients in the cooker first thing in the morning and programme it to produce the perfect dinner for you until lunchtime. Long cooking times allow the food to absorb the majority of the ingredients and infuse the meal with scent.

How to use it

If you have never used a slow cooker before, here's how to use it to make delectable and flavorful meals. To begin, position the unit on a firm surface close to the power supply. Make sure it's fully clean from the inside out before connecting it in. If not, use a soft dry towel to wipe it away. Remove the pot from the oven and rinse it in cold water. Before returning the cooking pot to the base unit, clean it thoroughly. Before you put everything back together, make sure the base is totally dry from the outside.

If the recipe calls for preheating the liquid, pour it into the slow cooker and cover it. The control panel can be used to set the time and mode. Allow time for it to heat up. To prepare the dinner, combine all of the ingredients in the slow cooker and keep the liquid level below the maximum fill line, as overfilling can result in leaking. Avoid adding the food because it will make a lot of froth while cooking.

Cover the slow cooker lid and secure it in the grooves of the base unit after adding the food. Set and seal the lid properly to help keep the pressure inside the pot constant. The vapours are trapped by the lid and returned to the food. As a result, the meal takes a bath in its own vapours. It's time to start cooking now that everything is in its proper location. Select a temperature mode from the control panel: 1. High, 2. Medium, or 3. Low. After adjusting the mode, you may choose the time and use the adjustment key to increase or reduce the number of minutes. The pot will begin to heat up in a few seconds and steadily cook the meal. It's time for you to unwind and wait for the slow cooker to finish its work.

The pot will automatically switch to "Keep Warm" mode after the completion beep. This setting keeps your meal warm until you check the gadget and turn it off. Remove the pot's lid and turn off the "Keep Warm" option. Give the cooked food a couple of gentle stirs. Then serve it up. Remember to clean the cooking pot after each cooking session. Because the inside pot is washable, it can be readily cleaned underwater. The metallic housing, on the other hand, should only be wiped with a soft cloth. After each session, it's also a good idea to wash the lid.

PART 2:

CHAPTER THREE: EASY APPETIZERS

SPINACH ARTICHOKE DIP

Preparation Time: 10 minutes
Cooking Time: 2 hours.
Serve: 8

Ingredients:

- 1 (14-ounce) can artichoke hearts, chopped
- 1 (10-ounce) package frozen spinach, chopped
- 1 small yellow onion, chopped
- 1 (8-ounce) package cream cheese, softened
- 1 (8-ounce) container sour cream
- 1/2 cup milk
- 1/4 cup mayonnaise
- 2/3 cup Parmesan cheese, grated
- 1/2 cup mozzarella cheese, grated
- 1/2 teaspoon garlic powder
- 1/2 teaspoon red pepper flakes
- 1/4 teaspoon black pepper
- 1/4 teaspoon salt

Directions:

1. Grease a 4 quarts slow cooker with cooking spray.
2. Add artichokes, sour cream and the rest of the ingredients.
3. Cover its lid and cook on LOW setting for 2 hours.
4. Stir well and serve warm.

Nutritional Value (Amount per Serving):

Calories 247; Fat 19.7g; Cholesterol 49mg; Carbohydrate 12.9g; Sugars 2.3g; Protein 7.5g

BEAN DIP

Preparation Time: 10 minutes
Cooking Time: 1 ½ hour.
Serve: 8

Ingredients:

* 16 ounces can refried beans
* 4 ½ ounces can mild green chiles
* 1 cup sour cream
* 1/3 cup salsa
* juice of 1 small lime
* 1/2 teaspoon garlic powder
* 1/2 teaspoon onion powder
* 1 teaspoon cumin
* 1 teaspoon chili powder
* 1 1/4 cups Mexican cheese
* salt to taste

Directions:

1. Add mild green chiles, refried beans, Mexican cheese, chilli powder, onion powder, garlic powder, lime juice, salsa, and sour cream to a slow cooker.
2. Cover its lid and cook on High heat setting for 1 ½ hour.
3. Uncover, adjust the seasoning with salt and stir well.
4. Garnish with enchiladas, burritos, and tortilla chips.
5. Serve warm.

Nutritional Value (Amount per Serving):

Calories 113; Fat 8g; Cholesterol 19mg; Carbohydrate 7.5g; Sugars 0.6g; Protein 3.9g

BOILED PEANUTS

Preparation Time: 10 minutes
Cooking Time: 7 hours.
Serve: 20

Ingredients:

* 6 cups raw peanuts
* 1/2 cup salt
* 2 ½ quarts water

Directions:

1. Rinse the peanuts under water, then transfer them to a slow cooker.
2. Add water and salt, then cook for 7 hours on a High heat setting.
3. Drain and serve.

Nutritional Value (Amount per Serving):

Calories 248; Fat 21.6g; Cholesterol 0mg; Carbohydrate 7.1g; Sugars 1.7g; Protein 11.3g

BACON STUFFED MUSHROOMS

Preparation Time: 10 minutes
Cooking Time: 5 hours.
Serve: 12

Ingredients:
- 20 large fresh mushrooms
- 2 packets of bacon, cooked and crumbled
- 2 blocks of cream cheese
- 1 tablespoon Worcestershire sauce
- 2 tablespoons Ranch Dressing mix
- 3 tablespoons of butter

Directions:
1. Cut of the mushroom stems and chop them.
2. Place the mushroom caps in a tray.
3. Mix the chopped mushroom stems with bacon, cream cheese, and ranch dressing mix in a bowl.
4. Stuff the mushrooms with cream cheese filling.
5. Place the stuffed mushrooms in the slow cooker.
6. Drizzle Worcestershire sauce and butter on top.
7. Cover its lid and cook for 5 hours on LOW heat.
8. Serve warm.

Nutritional Value (Amount per Serving):
Calories 167; Fat 13.5g; Cholesterol 37mg; Carbohydrate 5.8g; Dietary Fiber 1.2g; Sugars 3.7g; Protein 8g

LITTLE SMOKIES

Preparation Time: 10 minutes
Cooking Time: 3 hours.
Serve: 6

Ingredients:

- 2 (16 ounces) packages little smokies
- 1 cup bbq sauce
- ½ cup grape jelly
- 1 teaspoon sriracha

Directions:

1. Spread the smokies in a slow cooker.
2. Drizzle bbq sauce, sriracha and grape jelly on top.
3. Cover its lid and cook for 3 hours on LOW heat setting.
4. Serve warm.

Nutritional Value (Amount per Serving):

Calories 283; Fat 17.1g; Cholesterol 35mg; Carbohydrate 26.2g; Sugars 18.8g; Protein 6.1g

CHAPTER FOUR: BEEF, PORK, AND LAMB

BEEF BOURGUIGNON

Preparation Time: 10 minutes
Cooking Time: 10 hours. 11 minutes
Serve: 6

Ingredients:

* 5 slices bacon, chopped
* 3 pounds boneless beef chuck, diced
* 1 cup red cooking wine
* 2 cups chicken broth
* 1/2 cup tomato sauce
* 1/4 cup soy sauce
* 1/4 cup flour
* 3 garlic cloves, chopped
* 2 tablespoons thyme, chopped
* 5 medium carrots, sliced
* 1 pound baby potatoes, diced
* 8 ounces fresh mushrooms, sliced
* Chopped parsley for garnish

Directions:

1. Sauté bacon in a suitable skillet for 5 minutes until golden brown.
2. Transfer the bacon to a slow cooker.
3. Add beef to the same skillet and season with black pepper and salt.
4. Sear the beef for 3 minutes per side then transfer to a slow cooker.
5. Add red wine to the skillet and deglaze the pan then pour over the beef.
6. Stir in flour, soy sauce, tomato sauce and broth.
7. Add mushrooms, potatoes, carrots, thyme and garlic on top.
8. Cook on LOW heat settings for 10 hours.
9. Mix gently, garnish with parsley and serve warm.

Nutritional Value (Amount per Serving):

Calories 592; Fat 41.4g; Cholesterol 146mg; Carbohydrate 8.7g; Sugars 1.9g; Protein 43.6g

BEEF AND BROCCOLI

Preparation Time: 10 minutes
Cooking Time: 4 hours. 20 minutes
Serve: 2

Ingredients:

* 1 1/2 pound sirloin steak, thinly sliced
* 1 cup beef broth
* ½ cup soy sauce
* 1/2 cup brown sugar
* 3 tablespoons sesame oil
* 1 tablespoon sriracha
* 3 cloves garlic, minced
* 3 green onions, sliced
* 2 tablespoons cornstarch
* 2 cup broccoli florets
* Sesame seeds, for garnish
* Cooked jasmine rice, for serving

Directions:

1. Add steak, green onions, garlic, sriracha, sesame oil, brown sugar, soy sauce and beef broth to the slow cooker.
2. Cover its lid and cook on LOW heat settings for 4 hours.
3. Whisk cornstarch with water in a bowl.
4. Add broccoli and cornstarch mixture then cook for 20 minutes.
5. Garnish with green onions and sesame seeds.
6. Serve warm.

Nutritional Value (Amount per Serving):

Calories 537; Fat 21.8g; Cholesterol 153mg; Carbohydrate 28g; Sugars 20.4g; Protein 57g

MISSISSIPPI ROAST

Preparation Time: 10 minutes
Cooking Time: 4 hours.
Serve: 8

Ingredients:

- ½ cup beef broth
- ½ large onion, chopped
- 1 packet ranch seasoning
- 4 pound boneless beef chuck roast
- Salt, to taste
- Black pepper, to taste
- 1 cup pepperoncini, sliced
- 4 tablespoons butter
- Thick sliced bread, for serving

Directions:

1. Add onion, ranch seasoning and beef broth to the slow cooker.
2. Place the beef chuck roast in the cooker.
3. Add butter, pepperoncini, black pepper and salt on top.
4. Cover its lid and cook on HIGH setting for 4 hours.
5. Once done, shred the meat with a fork and return to the cooker.
6. Mix well and serve warm.

Nutritional Value (Amount per Serving):

Calories 478; Fat 20g; Cholesterol 218mg; Carbohydrate 1g; Sugars 0.4g; Protein 69.3g

BEEF AND BARLEY SOUP

Preparation Time: 10 minutes
Cooking Time: 8 hours. 15 minutes
Serve: 4

Ingredients:

- 1 ½ pound beef chuck, diced
- Salt, to taste
- Black pepper, to taste
- Olive oil, for drizzling
- 3 garlic cloves, minced
- 1 onion, diced
- 2 carrots, cut into half moons
- 2 teaspoon fresh thyme leaves
- 8 ounces cremini mushrooms, sliced
- 1/4 cup pearled barley
- 4 cups chicken stock
- 1 tablespoon soy sauce

Directions:

1. Pat dry the beef and rub them with black pepper and salt.
2. Sear the meat in a cast iron greased with oil for 5 minutes per side over medium heat.
3. Transfer the seared meat to a slow cooker.
4. Add onions, garlic, carrots, thyme, black pepper and salt to the same skillet.
5. Sauté the veggies for 5 minutes then transfer to the cooker.
6. Stir in rest of the ingredients, cover and cook for 8 hours on LOW heat.
7. Serve warm.

Nutritional Value (Amount per Serving):

Calories 425; Fat 10.9g; Cholesterol 152mg; Carbohydrate 19.9g; Sugars 5g; Protein 59.2g

PORK LOIN ROAST

Preparation Time: 10 minutes
Cooking Time: 5 hours. 41 minutes
Serve: 8

Ingredients:

- 5 pound pork loin, fillet, skinless
- 1 ½ tablespoon olive oil

Spice Rub
- 2 teaspoon paprika
- 2 teaspoon thyme
- 1 teaspoon garlic powder
- 1 teaspoon onion powder
- 1/2 teaspoon cayenne pepper
- 1/2 teaspoon pepper
- 2 teaspoon salt

Honey Butter Sauce
- ¾ cup honey
- ½ cup butter, unsalted
- 5 garlic cloves, minced
- 1/4 cup cider vinegar
- 1/2 teaspoon salt
- 1/2 teaspoon black pepper

Thickener
- 3 teaspoon corn flour
- A splash of water

Directions:

1. Mix the spices with 1 teaspoon oil in a bowl and rub this mixture over the pork,
2. Set a skillet with 1 tablespoon oil over medium heat and sear the pork for 5 minutes per side.
3. Transfer the pork to the slow cooker.
4. For honey butter sauce, sauté garlic with butter in a skillet for 1 minute.
5. Stir in rest of the sauce ingredients then cook for 30 seconds.
6. Pour this sauce over the pork, cover its lid and cook for 5 hours on LOW heat setting.
7. Mix corn flour with water and pour into the cooker.
8. Cover and continue cooking for 30 minutes.
9. Mix well and serve warm.

Nutritional Value (Amount per Serving):

Calories 474; Fat 21.2g; Cholesterol 155mg; Carbohydrate 27g; Sugars 26.2g; Protein 43.9g

PORK CASSEROLE

Preparation Time: 10 minutes
Cooking Time: 6 hours. 26 minutes
Serve: 4

Ingredients:

- 1 tablespoon vegetable oil
- 4 pork shoulder steaks, cut into chunks
- 1 onion, chopped
- 1 leek, chopped
- 1 carrot, chopped
- 1 chicken stock cube
- 2 teaspoon Dijon mustard
- 1 tablespoon cider vinegar
- 2 teaspoon corn flour
- 1 tablespoon honey

Bundle of herbs
- 2 bay leaves
- 3 sage leaves
- 4 thyme sprigs

Directions:

1. Set a skillet greased with oil over medium heat.
2. Sear the pork for 5 minutes per side until golden brown.
3. Transfer the pork to the slow cooker.
4. Add leeks and onion to the same skillet and cook for 6 minutes.
5. Transfer the veggies to the slow cooker along with seasonings, vinegar, mustard, stock cube, herbs and carrot.
6. Cover it lid and cook for 6 hours on HIGH heat setting.
7. Meanwhile, mix corn flour with honey in a bowl and add to the cooker.
8. Mi well and cook for 10 minutes with stirring.
9. Serve warm.

Nutritional Value (Amount per Serving):

Calories 525; Fat 31.9g; Cholesterol 161mg; Carbohydrate 12.9g; Sugars 7.2g; Protein 44.4g

TEXAS PULLED PORK

Preparation Time: 10 minutes
Cooking Time: 6 hours. 6 minutes
Serve: 8

Ingredients:

- 1 teaspoon vegetable oil
- 1 (4 pounds) pork shoulder roast
- 1 cup barbeque sauce
- ½ cup apple cider vinegar
- ½ cup chicken broth
- ¼ cup light brown sugar
- 1 tablespoon prepared yellow mustard
- 1 tablespoon Worcestershire sauce
- 1 tablespoon chili powder
- 1 onion, chopped
- 2 large garlic cloves, crushed
- 1 ½ teaspoons dried thyme
- 8 hamburger buns, split
- 2 tablespoons butter

Directions:

1. Grease the slow cooker's pot with oil and place the pork roast in it.
2. Add onion, thyme, garlic, chili powder, Worcestershire sauce, mustard, brown sugar, apple cider vinegar and barbecue sauce.
3. Mix well, cover its lid and cook for 6 hours on High heat setting.
4. Shred the cook pork with two forks and mix the meat with the sauce.
5. Melt butter in a skillet and toast the buns for 2-3 minutes per side.
6. Stuff the buns with shredded pork and serve.

Nutritional Value (Amount per Serving):

Calories 444; Fat 23g; Cholesterol 68mg; Carbohydrate 38.2g; Sugars 15.8g; Protein 18.9g

GARLIC BALSAMIC PORK LOIN

Preparation Time: 10 minutes
Cooking Time: 3 hours. 10 minutes
Serve: 6

Ingredients:

* 3 pounds pork loin
* 1 teaspoon salt
* 1 teaspoon paprika
* ½ teaspoon onion powder
* ¼ teaspoon fresh ground pepper
* ⅓ cup chicken broth
* 4 tablespoons olive oil
* 3 tablespoons balsamic vinegar
* 5 cloves garlic, smashed
* ½ tablespoon Italian seasoning

Directions:

1. Mix black pepper, onion powder, paprika and salt in a small bowl.
2. Rub this mixture over the pork liberally.
3. Set a skillet with 1 tablespoon oil over medium heat.
4. Sear the pork for 5 minutes per side then transfer to the slow cooker
5. Blend garlic with remaining oil, vinegar and seasoning in a blender until smooth.
6. Pour and brush this mixture over the pork and pour the broth around the pork.
7. Cover its lid and cook for 3 hours on HIGH heat setting.
8. Slice the pork and serve warm.

Nutritional Value (Amount per Serving):

Servings: 6; Calories 642; Fat 41.4g; Cholesterol 182mg; Carbohydrate 1.5g; Sugars 0.3g; Protein 62.5g

SLOW COOKED PORK CHOPS

Preparation Time: 10 minutes
Cooking Time: 2 hours. 6 minutes
Serve: 4

Ingredients:

* 2 tablespoons olive oil
* 4 boneless pork chops
* Salt, to taste
* Black pepper, to taste
* 2 peaches, sliced
* 1 red onion, sliced
* ¼ teaspoon crushed red pepper flakes
* 3 sprigs fresh thyme
* 1/2 cup chicken broth
* 2 tablespoons apple cider vinegar
* 1 tablespoon brown sugar
* Cooked white rice, for serving
* Freshly chopped parsley, for garnish

Directions:

1. Rub the black pepper and salt over the pork chops.
2. Set a skillet greased with oil over medium-high heat.
3. Sear the pork chops for 2-3 minutes per side.
4. Add peaches, broth and rest of the ingredients to the slow cooker.
5. Place the seared pork chops over this mixture.
6. Cover and cook for almost 2 hours on HIGH heat setting.
7. Garnish with herbs and serve warm.

Nutritional Value (Amount per Serving):

Calories 589; Fat 18.9g; Cholesterol 243mg; Carbohydrate 12.1g; Sugars 10.4g; Protein 88.4g

BROWN SUGAR GLAZED HAM

Preparation Time: 10 minutes
Cooking Time: 6 hours. 7 minutes
Serve: 8

Ingredients:

* 1 cup packed brown sugar
* 1/3 cup honey
* 1 cup apple cider
* 1/4 cup Dijon mustard
* 1/2 teaspoon smoked paprika
* 1/2 teaspoon garlic powder
* Salt, to taste
* Black pepper, to taste
* 1 (4-6 pound) spiral cut ham

Directions:

1. Mix garlic powder, paprika, mustard, cider, honey and sugar in a saucepan.
2. Stir in black pepper and salt then cook for 7 minutes with stirring.
3. Place the ham in the slow cooker and slightly separate the slices.
4. Pour the prepare glaze on top and brush well.
5. Cover its lid and cook for 6 hours on LOW heat.
6. Serve warm.

Nutritional Value (Amount per Serving):

Calories 502; Fat 19.9g; Cholesterol 129mg; Carbohydrate 42.4g; Sugars 32.7g; Protein 38.1g

SLOW COOKER LAMB SHOULDER

Preparation Time: 10 minutes
Cooking Time: 6 hours.
Serve: 6

Ingredients:

- 4 ½ pounds lamb shoulder
- 2 cups lamb stock
- 1 cup red wine
- 4 tablespoons corn flour
- 4 garlic cloves, sliced
- 4 sprigs rosemary
- 1 teaspoon blackcurrant jam
- 1 large onion, chopped
- 1 teaspoon salt
- 1 teaspoon black pepper
- 1 large carrot, chopped

Directions:

1. Add chopped vegetables, rosemary and 3 tablespoons corn flour to the slow cooker.
2. Poke some holes in the lamb shoulder and stuff each hole with garlic then rub with black pepper and salt.
3. Set the prepared lamb in the slow cooker and pour the wine and stock around it.
4. Cover its lid and cook for 5 ½ hours on HIGH heat.
5. Transfer the slow cooked lamb to a roasting pan and bake for 20 minutes at 350 degrees F.
6. Meanwhile, add corn flour to the leftover gravy in the slow cooker.
7. Mix it well then transfer to a saucepan and cook until it thickens.
8. Stir in jam and mix well.
9. Place the roasted lamb to a plate and slice.
10. Pour the jam sauce on top and serve warm.

Nutritional Value (Amount per Serving):

Calories 406; Fat 12.3g; Cholesterol 147mg; Carbohydrate 12.9g; Sugars 3g; Protein 47.1g

LAMB WITH OLIVES AND POTATOES

Preparation Time: 10 minutes
Cooking Time: 3 hours. 40 minutes
Serve: 6

Ingredients:

* 1 ¼ pounds small potatoes, halved
* 4 large shallots, cut into 1/2-inch wedges
* 3 garlic cloves, minced
* 1 tablespoon grated lemon zest
* 2 tablespoons lemon juice
* 3 sprigs rosemary
* Salt and black pepper, to taste
* 4 tablespoons all-purpose flour
* 3/4 cup chicken broth
* 3 1/2 pounds lamb shanks, cut into 1 1/2-inch pieces
* 2 tablespoons olive oil
* 1/2 cup dry white wine
* 1 cup pitted green olives, halved

Directions:

1. Toss potatoes with rosemary, lemon zest, garlic and shallots in a slow cooker.
2. Add black pepper, salt, 1 tablespoon flour and broth on top.
3. Rub the lamb with black pepper and salt.
4. Spread 3 tablespoons flour in a plate and coat the lamb with it then shake off the excess.
5. Set a skillet with cooking oil over medium high heat.
6. Sear the lamb for 5 minutes per side until golden brown.
7. Transfer the lamb to the slow cooker.
8. Add wine to the same skillet and cook for 2 minutes then transfer to the cooker.
9. Cover its lid and cook for 3 ½ hours on HIGH heat setting.
10. Add olives, cover and cook for 20 minutes.
11. Drizzle lemon juice, black pepper and salt on top.
12. Serve warm.

Nutritional Value (Amount per Serving):

Calories 479; Fat 18.2g; Cholesterol 179mg; Carbohydrate 15.2g; Sugars 1g; Protein 57.6g

CHAPTER FIVE: POULTRY

HONEY GARLIC CHICKEN

Preparation Time: 10 minutes
Cooking Time: 3 hours. 10 minutes
Serve: 6

Ingredients:

Chicken
* 6 large chicken thighs, bone-in
* 1 tablespoon olive oil

Rub
* 1 teaspoon paprika
* 1/2 teaspoon brown sugar
* 1/2 teaspoon garlic powder
* 1/2 teaspoon onion powder
* 1/8 teaspoon cayenne pepper
* 1 teaspoon coarse salt
* 1/4 teaspoon black cracked pepper

Honey Garlic Butter Sauce
* 1/2 cup honey
* 1/2 cup unsalted butter
* 6 cloves garlic, chopped
* 2 tablespoons soy sauce
* 2 tablespoons rice wine vinegar
* 1 pinch of salt
* ½ teaspoon cracked black pepper

Additional
* ¼ cup water
* 2 teaspoons cornstarch

Directions:

1. Pat dry the chicken with paper towel.
2. Mix all the ingredients for spice rub and oil in a bowl.
3. Rub this mixture over the chicken liberally.
4. Set a skillet with ½ tablespoon oil over medium heat.
5. Sear the chicken for 2 minutes per side.
6. Transfer the chicken thighs to a slow cooker.
7. Sauté garlic with butter in the same skillet for 1 minute.
8. Add rest of the butter sauce ingredients then cook for 1 minute on simmer.
9. Pour this sauce over the chicken, cover its lid and cook for 3 hours on HIGH heat setting.
10. Transfer the chicken to a plate and keep it cover.
11. Pour the leftover drippings to a saucepan.
12. Mix corn flour with ¼ cup water in a bowl then pour in to saucepan.
13. Cook for 2 minutes with stirring until it thickens.
14. Place the chicken in a baking sheet and pour the sauce on top.
15. Broil the saucy chicken for 2 minutes.
16. Slice and serve warm.

Nutritional Value (Amount per Serving):

Calories 388; Fat 21.1g; Cholesterol 124mg; Carbohydrate 18.3g; Sugars 17.8g; Protein 30.8g

HERBED SLOW-COOKER CHICKEN

Preparation Time: 10 minutes
Cooking Time: 5 hours.
Serve: 4

Ingredients:

- 1 tablespoon olive oil
- 1 teaspoon paprika
- 1/2 teaspoon garlic powder
- 1/2 teaspoon seasoned salt
- 1/2 teaspoon dried thyme
- 1/2 teaspoon dried basil
- 1/2 teaspoon pepper
- 1/2 teaspoon browning sauce
- 4 bone-in chicken breast halves
- 1/2 cup chicken broth

Directions:

1. Mix olive oil, paprika, garlic powder, salt, thyme, browning sauce, basil and black pepper in a bowl.
2. Rub this mixture over the chicken liberally then place it in the slow cooker.
3. Pour the broth around the chicken, cover it with a lid and cook for 5 hours on LOW heat.
4. Serve warm.

Nutritional Value (Amount per Serving):

Calories 269; Fat 12.8g; Cholesterol 120mg; Carbohydrate 1.9g; Sugars 1.2g ; Protein 34.8g

CHICKEN AND POTATOES

Preparation Time: 10 minutes
Cooking Time: 2 hours. 1 minute
Serve: 4

Ingredients:

* 1 pound baby Yukon gold potatoes, quartered
* 1 pound baby carrots, dices
* 1 ½ pounds boneless chicken breasts
* 4 tablespoons unsalted butter
* 3 cloves garlic minced
* 2 ½ teaspoons Italian seasoning
* ½ teaspoon kosher salt
* ¼ teaspoon black pepper
* Zest and juice of 1 medium lemon
* ¼ cup Parmesan cheese, grated
* Chopped fresh parsley for serving

Directions:

5. Spread the potatoes in a 6 quart slow cooker.
6. Place the carrots and chicken on top.
7. Sauté garlic with butter in a pan for 1 minute.
8. Stir in black pepper, salt, Italian seasoning, lemon juice and zest and lemon juice.
9. Mix well the pour over this sauce over the chicken and cover it with a lid.
10. Cook for 2 hours on HIGH heat setting.
11. Flip the chicken once cooked halfway through.
12. Garnish with parsley and parmesan.
13. Serve warm.

Nutritional Value (Amount per Serving):

Calories 515; Fat 25.6g; Cholesterol 185mg; Carbohydrate 18.1g; Sugars 6g; Protein 51.7g

SLOW COOKER CHICKEN WITH GARLIC

Preparation Time: 10 minutes
Cooking Time: 3 hours. 4 minutes
Serve: 4

Ingredients:

- * 1 (28-ounce) can cans cannellini beans, drained
- * 20 garlic cloves, smashed
- * 1/3 cup white wine
- * 2 tablespoons olive oil
- * 1 tablespoon white wine vinegar
- * 2 fresh thyme sprigs
- * ½ teaspoon red-pepper flakes
- * Salt and black pepper, to taste
- * 2 pounds bone-in chicken thighs
- * ½ lemon, juiced
- * 2 scallions, trimmed, sliced
- * ½ cup fresh parsley, chopped

Directions:

1. Add beans, red pepper flakes, thyme, vinegar, oil, wine and garlic to a 6 quart slow cooker.
2. Place the chicken in the cooker and drizzle salt and black pepper on top.
3. Cover it with a lid and cook for 3 hours on HIGH heat setting.
4. Transfer the chicken to a roasting pan and broil for 4 minutes.
5. Add lemon juice, parsley and scallions to the beans mixture.
6. Transfer the beans to the serving bowl and top them with broiled chicken.
7. Serve warm.

Nutritional Value (Amount per Serving):

Calories 401; Fat 26g; Cholesterol 98mg; Carbohydrate 17.1g; Sugars 1.1g; Protein 22.1g

SLOW COOKER CHICKEN CHILI

Preparation Time: 10 minutes
Cooking Time: 7 hours. 15 minutes
Serve: 6

Ingredients:

* 2 (14 ounce) cans petite tomatoes, drained
* 2 boneless chicken breasts
* 2 cups chicken broth
* 2 (8 ounces) cans tomato sauce
* 1/2 cup yellow onion, diced
* 1 large green bell pepper, chopped
* 1 (14 ounce) can corn, drained
* 1 (14 ounce) can black beans, drained
* 1 jalapeño, minced
* 1 teaspoon salt
* 2 teaspoons dried oregano
* 2 teaspoons chili powder
* 1 tablespoon ground cumin
* 1 tablespoon garlic, minced
* 4 ounces light cream cheese

Directions:

1. Add black beans, and rest of the ingredients, except the cream cheese to a slow cooker.
2. Cover this mixture with a lid and cook for 7 hours on LOW heat.
3. Shred the cooked chicken with two forks and return to the cooker.
4. Add cream cheese, cover and cook for 15 minutes
5. Garnish with shredded cheese, and cilantro.
6. Serve warm.

Nutritional Value (Amount per Serving):

Calories 465; Fat 9.9g; Cholesterol 64mg; Carbohydrate 59.3g; Sugars 10.2g; Protein 38.2g

CHAPTER SIX: SEAFOOD

SEAFOOD CIOPPINO

Preparation Time: 10 minutes
Cooking Time: 5 ½ hours.
Serve: 4

Ingredients:

* 1 can (28 ounces) diced tomatoes, undrained
* 2 medium onions, chopped
* 3 celery ribs, chopped
* 8 ounces clam juice
* 1 can (6 ounces) tomato paste
* 1/2 cup white wine
* 5 garlic cloves, minced
* 1 tablespoon red wine vinegar
* 1 tablespoon olive oil
* 2 teaspoons Italian seasoning
* 1 bay leaf
* 1/2 teaspoon sugar
* 1 pound haddock fillets, diced
* 1 pound uncooked shrimp, peeled and deveined
* 1 can (6 ounces) clams, chopped, undrained
* 1 can (6 ounces) lump crabmeat, drained
* 2 tablespoons fresh parsley, minced

Directions:

1. Add tomatoes and rest of the ingredients except the seafood.
2. Cover this tomato mixture with the lid and cook for 5 hours on LOW heat setting.
3. Add the reserved seafood, cover again and cook for 30 minutes on LOW heat.
4. Garnish with parsley and serve warm.

Nutritional Value (Amount per Serving):

Calories 449; Fat 7.9g; Cholesterol 353mg; Carbohydrate 25g; Sugars 11.4g; Protein 62.9g

SLOW COOKER SEAFOOD STEW

Preparation Time: 10 minutes
Cooking Time: 7 hours.
Serve: 6

Ingredients:

* 1 (28 ounces) can tomatoes, crushed
* 4 cups vegetable broth
* 3 garlic cloves , minced
* 1 tablespoon tomato paste
* 1 pound yellow potatoes , diced
* 1/2 cup white onion, chopped
* 1 teaspoon dried thyme
* 1 teaspoon dried basil
* 1 teaspoon dried oregano
* 1/2 teaspoon celery salt
* 1/4 teaspoon crush red pepper flakes
* 1/8 teaspoon cayenne pepper
* salt and pepper to taste
* 2 pounds seafood
* 1 handful of parsley, chopped

Directions:

5. Add diced potatoes and rest of the ingredients, except the seafood, to the slow cooker.
6. Cover this mixture with the lid and cook for 6 hours on LOW heat.
7. Add seafood, cover again and cook for 1 hour no HIGH heat.
8. Garnish with parsley and serve with bread.

Nutritional Value (Amount per Serving):

Calories 404; Fat 4.1g; Cholesterol 58mg; Carbohydrate 73.4g; Sugars 3.1g; Protein 26.9g

SHRIMP SCAMPI

Preparation Time: 10 minutes
Cooking Time: 2 hours.
Serve: 4

Ingredients:
* 2 pounds shrimp frozen, deveined and peeled
* Salt and black pepper to taste
* 1 tablespoon garlic salt
* 2 lemons, squeezed
* 1 cup chicken broth
* 2 tablespoons fresh parsley
* ½ cup parmesan cheese, grated

To serve:
* 16 ounces angel hair pasta, cooked

Directions:
1. Add pasta, half of the parmesan, shrimp and rest of the ingredients to the slow cooker.
2. Cover this mixture with a lid and cook for 2 hours on HIGH Heat setting.
3. Drizzle remaining cheese on top and serve warm with the pasta.

Nutritional Value (Amount per Serving):

Calories 410; Fat 4.7g; Cholesterol 165mg; Carbohydrate 64.1g; Sugars 0.7g ; Protein 26.6g

SHRIMP BOIL

Preparation Time: 10 minutes
Cooking Time: 5 hours.
Serve: 2

Ingredients:

- 1/4 cup Old Bay seasoning
- 2 tablespoons lemon juice
- 1 tablespoon hot sauce
- 1 1/2 pounds small red potatoes
- 1 medium sweet onion, cut into wedges
- 1 head garlic, halved
- 2 bay leaves
- 1 (12.8-ounce) package smoked andouille sausage, diced
- 3 ears corn, each into 3 pieces
- 2 pounds medium shrimp
- 2 tablespoons parsley leaves, chopped

Directions:

1. Mix 6 cup water with hot sauce, lemon juice, and old bay seasoning in a slow cooker pot.
2. Stir in potatoes, garlic, bay leaves and onion then cover and cook for 4 hours on LOW heat.
3. Add corn and sausage then cook again for 30 minutes on HIGH heat.
4. Stir in shrimp, cover and continue cooking for 30 minutes on HIGH heat.
5. Garnish with parsley and serve warm.

Nutritional Value (Amount per Serving):

Calories 384; Fat 7.8g; Cholesterol 249mg; Carbohydrate 38.8g; Sugars 5.2g; Protein 42.7g

SAUSAGE AND SHRIMP GUMBO

Preparation Time: 10 minutes
Cooking Time: 6 hours. 40 minutes
Serve: 4

Ingredients:

* 1 tablespoon olive oil
* 1 bell pepper, diced
* 1/2 cup diced onion
* 2 stalks celery, diced
* 2-3 cloves garlic, minced
* 14 ounces andouille sausage, sliced
* 1 (15 ounces) can diced tomatoes
* 4 cups chicken broth
* 1-2 teaspoons Cajun seasoning
* 2 bay leaves
* 1/2 teaspoon dried oregano
* 1/2 teaspoon dried thyme
* 1/2 teaspoon dried basil
* 1 teaspoon hot sauce
* 1 tablespoon Worcestershire sauce
* 1/4 cup cornstarch
* 1/4 cup water
* 10 ounces shrimp, peeled and deveined
* Salt and pepper, to taste
* Hot cooked rice, for serving

Directions:

1. Sauté sausage, garlic, celery, onion and pepper with oil in a large skillet for 10 minutes.
2. Add tomatoes, Worcestershire sauce, hot sauce, spices and broth to the slow cooker.
3. Stir in sausage mixture, cover and cook for 6 hours on LOW heat.
4. Mix ¼ cup cornstarch with water and pour into the cooker.
5. Add shrimp, cover again and cook for 30 minutes with occasional stirring.
6. Serve warm.

Nutritional Value (Amount per Serving):

Calories 379; Fat 22.4g; Cholesterol 137mg; Carbohydrate 15.5g; Sugars 4.9g; Protein 27.7g

CHAPTER SEVEN:
VEGETABLES, GRAINS AND LEGUMES

SLOW COOKER AUBERGINES

Preparation Time: 10 minutes
Cooking Time: 8 hours.
Serve: 4

Ingredients:

- 4 tablespoons olive oil
- 1 red onion, sliced
- 2 garlic cloves, crushed
- 1 pound aubergines
- 10 1/2 ounces ripe tomatoes, quartered
- 1 small fennel bulb, sliced
- 1 ounce sundried tomatoes
- 1 teaspoon coriander seeds

Dressing
- 1 bunch flat leaf parsley, chopped
- 1 bunch basil, chopped
- 1 bunch chives, chopped
- 2 tablespoons olive oil
- juice 1 lemon
- 2 teaspoon capers

Topping
- 3 1/2 ounces feta cheese
- 1 ounce toasted flaked almonds

Serve
- crusty bread

Directions:

1. Toss garlic with onions in a slow cooker.
2. Brush the aubergines slices with remaining oil and place them over the onions.
3. Add tomatoes, sun dried tomatoes, fennel slices, black pepper, salt and coriander seeds on top.
4. Cover these layers with the lid and cook for 8 hours on LOW heat.
5. Meanwhile, puree the dressing ingredients in a blender.
6. Pour the dressing over the veggies then drizzle the feta cheese and almond on top.
7. Serve warm with bread.

Nutritional Value (Amount per Serving):

Calories 283; Fat 20.2g; Cholesterol 22mg; Carbohydrate 23g; Sugars 12.6g; Protein 7.9g

SLOW COOKER RATATOUILLE

Preparation Time: 10 minutes
Cooking Time: 6 hours. 19 minutes
Serve: 4

Ingredients:
* 2 tablespoons olive oil
* 1 red onion, sliced
* 2 garlic cloves, minced
* 2 large aubergines, cut into cubes
* 3 courgettes, cut into cubes
* 3 mixed peppers, cut into cubes
* 1 tablespoon tomato purée
* 6 large tomatoes, chopped
* 1 small bunch of basil, chopped
* 2 thyme sprigs
* 14 ounces can plum tomatoes
* 1 tablespoon red wine vinegar
* 1 teaspoon brown sugar
* Sourdough bread, to serve

Directions:
1. Sauté onion with oil in a skillet for 8 minutes.
2. Stir in garlic and cook for 1 minutes then add aubergines.
3. Cook for 5 minutes then add peppers and courgettes and cook for 5 minutes.
4. Transfer this mixture to a slow cooker.
5. Stir in salt, sugar, vinegar, tomatoes, herbs, and tomato puree.
6. Cover this mixture with a lid and cook for 6 hours on LOW heat.
7. Stir gently and garnish with basil.
8. Serve warm.

Nutritional Value (Amount per Serving):
Calories 309; Fat 14.8g; Cholesterol 0mg; Carbohydrate 39.8g; Sugars 21.9g; Protein 8.7g

AUBERGINE AND CHICKPEA STEW

Preparation Time: 10 minutes
Cooking Time: 8 hours. 21 minutes
Serve: 6

Ingredients:

- 8 ounces dried chickpeas, soaked
- 2 tablespoons olive oil
- 2 onions, sliced
- 6 garlic cloves, crushed
- 1 tablespoon baharat spice
- 1 teaspoon ground cinnamon
- 1 small bunch of parsley, chopped
- 3 medium aubergines, sliced
- 2 x 14 ounces cans tomatoes, chopped
- 1 lemon , juiced
- 1 ounce pine nuts , toasted, to serve
- Pitta bread, to serve

Directions:

1. Add chickpeas and water to a suitable pan then cook for 10 minutes then drain.
2. Sauté onions with oil in a skillet for 10 minutes.
3. Stir in cinnamon, baharat and garlic then cook for 1 minute.
4. Transfer this mixture, to the slow cooker along with tomatoes, a cup of water, aubergines, parsley and chickpeas.
5. Add seasonings, cover and cook for 8 hours on Low heat with occasional stirring.
6. Garnish with lemon juice, parsley, pine nuts and oil.
7. Serve warm with bread.

Nutritional Value (Amount per Serving):

Calories 317; Fat 13.1g; Cholesterol 0mg; Carbohydrate 44.5g; Sugars 15.3g; Protein 11.4g

MUSHROOMS WITH RICOTTA AND PESTO

Preparation Time: 10 minutes
Cooking Time: 4 hours.
Serve: 4

Ingredients:

- 5 tablespoon olive oil
- 16 chestnut mushrooms, stems removed
- 9 ounces tub ricotta
- 2 tablespoons green pesto
- 2 garlic cloves, chopped
- ½ ounces freshly parmesan, grated
- 1 tablespoon pesto
- 2 tablespoons chopped fresh parsley, to serve
- ¼ cup broth

Directions:

1. Grease a slow cooker pot with 1 tablespoon oil.
2. Mix garlic with pesto and ricotta in a bowl.
3. Divide this mixture into the mushrooms and place them in the cooker.
4. Drizzle parmesan cheese and parsley on top of the mushrooms.
5. Pour the broth around the mushrooms, cover and cook for 4 hours on HIGH heat.
6. Serve warm.

Nutritional Value (Amount per Serving):

Calories 355; Fat 32.6g; Cholesterol 13mg; Carbohydrate 7.9g; Sugars 0.7g; Protein 11.3g

SWEET POTATO AND COCONUT CURRY

Preparation Time: 10 minutes
Cooking Time: 8 hours. 19 minutes
Serve: 4

Ingredients:
* 4 tablespoons olive oil
* 2 large onions, halved and sliced
* 3 garlic cloves, crushed
* 1 thumb-sized piece root ginger, peeled
* 1 teaspoon paprika
* ½ teaspoon cayenne
* 2 red chilllies, sliced
* 2 red peppers, sliced
* 9 ounces red cabbage, shredded
* 2 pounds sweet potatoes, peeled and chopped
* 10 ½ ounces passata
* 1 ½ cups coconut milk
* 2 tablespoons peanut butter

Directions:
1. Sauté onion with 1 tablespoon olive oil in a skillet for 10 minutes.
2. Stir in ginger, garlic, cayenne and paprika then cook for 1 minute.
3. Transfer this onion mixture to the slow cooker.
4. Sauté cabbage with 1 tablespoon oil, red pepper and chili in the same skillet for 5 minutes.
5. Transfer the cabbage mixture to the slow cooker.
6. Sauté sweet potatoes with remaining oil in the same skillet for 3 minutes.
7. Transfer the potatoes to the slow cooker.
8. Stir in coconut milk, and passata, cover and cook for 8 hours on LOW heat.
9. Add peanut butter, black pepper and salt.
10. Garnish with coriander then serve with couscous.
11. Enjoy.

Nutritional Value (Amount per Serving):
Calories 391; Fat 21.5g; Cholesterol 0mg; Carbohydrate 47.6g; Sugars 5.9g; Protein 5.6g

SPICED CARROT AND LENTIL SOUP

Preparation Time: 10 minutes
Cooking Time: 8 hours. 1 minute
Serve: 6

Ingredients:

* 2 teaspoon cumin seeds
* pinch chilli flakes
* 2 tablespoons olive oil
* 1 2/3 pounds carrots, grated
* 7 ounces split red lentils
* 4 cups hot vegetable stock
* ½ cup milk

Directions:

1. Roast cumin seeds with a pinch of chili flakes in a pan for 1 minute.
2. Transfer half of this mixture to the slow cooker and keep the other half aside.
3. Add 2 tablespoons oil, carrots, stocks and rest of the ingredients.
4. Cover this mixture with a lid and cook for 6-8 hours on LOW heat.
5. Puree the cooked lentil soup using an immersion blender until smooth.
6. Garnish with reserved spices and serve.

Nutritional Value (Amount per Serving):

Calories 107; Fat 4.4g; Cholesterol 0mg; Carbohydrate 14.3g; Sugars 0.3g; Protein 3.2g

SLOW COOKER BEANS

Preparation Time: 10 minutes
Cooking Time: 5 hours. 6 minutes
Serve: 4

Ingredients:

- 1 tablespoon olive oil
- 1 onion , thinly sliced
- 2 garlic cloves , chopped
- 1 tablespoon white or red wine vinegar
- 1 heaped tablespoon soft brown sugar
- 1 (14 ounces) can pinto beans , drained+
- 2/3 ounces passata
- 1 small bunch coriander , chopped

Directions:

1. Sauté onion with oil in a skillet for 5 minutes.
2. Stir in garlic and cook for 1 minute then add vinegar.
3. Cook for 1 minutes and transfer to the slow cooker.
4. Add black pepper, passata and beans, cover and cook for 5 hours on LOW heat.
5. Garnish with coriander and serve warm.

Nutritional Value (Amount per Serving):

Calories 232; Fat 4.2g; Cholesterol 0mg; Carbohydrate 37.6g; Sugars 2.3g; Protein 10.7g

SLOW COOKER MASALA LENTILS

Preparation Time: 10 minutes
Cooking Time: 4 hours.
Serve: 4

Ingredients:

* 1 onion, chopped
* 3 cloves garlic, minced
* 1 tablespoon minced, fresh ginger
* 1 ½ cups tomatoes, diced
* 2 cups brown lentils
* 4 cups vegetable broth
* 1/4 cup tomato paste
* 2 tablespoons tamarind paste
* 3/4 teaspoon salt
* 1 1/2 teaspoon garam masala
* A few shakes black pepper
* 3/4 cup cashew cream
* Cooked rice, for serving
* Chopped fresh cilantro, for serving

Directions:

1. Add lentils, tomatoes and rest of the ingredients, except the cashew cream.
2. Cover this mixture with a lid and cook for 4 hours on HIGH heat.
3. Stir in cashew cream, mix well and garnish with cilantro.
4. Serve warm.

Nutritional Value (Amount per Serving):

Calories 466; Fat 5.5g; Cholesterol 8mg; Carbohydrate 72.9g; Sugars 11.9g; Protein 32.1g

MEDITERRANEAN BULGUR AND LENTILS

Preparation Time: 10 minutes
Cooking Time: 4 hours. 15 minutes
Serve: 4

Ingredients:

* 1 cup uncooked bulgur wheat
* ½ cup dried lentils, sorted, rinsed
* 1 teaspoon ground cumin
* ¼ teaspoon salt
* 3 cloves garlic, chopped
* 1 can (15.25 ounces) kernel corn, drained
* 2 cans (14 ounces) vegetable broth
* 2 medium tomatoes, chopped
* ½ cup drained pitted kalamata olives
* 1 cup crumbled feta cheese

Directions:

1. Add broth, corn, garlic, salt, cumin, lentils and bulgur to a slow cooker.
2. Cover this mixture with the lid and cook for 4 hours on LOW heat.
3. Stir in olives and tomatoes, cover and cook for 15 minutes at HIGH heat.
4. Garnish with cheese and serve warm.

Nutritional Value (Amount per Serving):

Calories 327; Fat 4.6g; Cholesterol 4mg; Carbohydrate 53.2g; Sugars 4.6g; Protein 19.8g

VEGETABLE BEAN SOUP

Preparation Time: 10 minutes
Cooking Time: 8 hours.
Serve: 4

Ingredients:

    1pound dried Great Northern beans, soaked, drained
- 3 carrots, diced
- 2 stalks celery, diced
- 1 onion, diced
- 3 garlic cloves, minced
- 1/2 teaspoon dried rubbed sage
- 4 cups vegetable broth
- 2 cups water
- Salt and black pepper to taste

Directions:

1. Soak beans in water overnight then drain.
2. Transfer the beans, sage, garlic, onion, celery and carrot to a slow cooker.
3. Pour in water and broth then cover it with the lid.
4. Cook on HIGH heat setting for 8 hours.
5. Adjust seasoning with black pepper and salt then serve warm.

Nutritional Value (Amount per Serving):

Calories 305; Fat 1.8g; Cholesterol 0mg; Carbohydrate 53.2g; Sugars 4.6g; Protein 20.4g

BEAN AND BARLEY STEW

Preparation Time: 10 minutes
Cooking Time: 8 hours.
Serve: 4

Ingredients:
* 8 cups chicken broth
* 1 pound dried beans, rinsed
* 2 teaspoons salt
* ½ teaspoon black pepper
* 3 stalks celery, diced
* 2 carrots, diced
* 2 garlic cloves, minced
* 1 yellow onion, chopped
* 1 bay leaf
* 2 sprigs fresh thyme
* 8 ounces dried barley
* 8 ounces baby spinach
* Toasted crusty bread, for serving

Directions:
1. Add water, thyme, onions, carrots and rest of the ingredients except the spinach to a slow cooker.
2. Cover this mixture with the lid and cook for 8 hours on LOW heat.
3. Stir in spinach and serve warm.

Nutritional Value (Amount per Serving):
Calories 459; Fat 9.3g; Cholesterol 0mg; Carbohydrate 75.2g; Sugars 4.9g; Protein 27.2g

BEAN SOUP WITH SWEET POTATOES

Preparation Time: 10 minutes
Cooking Time: 8 hours. 6 minutes
Serve: 4

Ingredients:

- 1 teaspoon olive oil
- 1 yellow onion, chopped
- 3 garlic cloves, minced
- 2 (14 ounces) cans red kidney beans, drained
- 1 pound sweet potato, peeled and diced
- 1 cup dry quinoa
- 1 (14-ounces) can petite tomatoes, diced
- 1 ½ teaspoons Italian seasoning
- ½ teaspoon salt
- ½ teaspoon black pepper
- 6 ½ cups vegetable broth
- 2 cups spinach leaves
- 1/4 cup parsley, minced
- Hot sauce to taste

Directions:

1. Sauté onions with oil in a skillet for 5 minutes.
2. Stir in garlic and cook for 1 minute.
3. Transfer this onion mixture to the slow cooker.
4. Add black pepper, salt, Italian seasoning, tomatoes, quinoa, sweet potato, kidney beans and vegetable broth.
5. Cover this mixture with the lid and cook for 8 hours on LOW heat.
6. Ad parsley, spinach and hot sauce.
7. Serve warm.

Nutritional Value (Amount per Serving):

Calories 374; Fat 5g; Cholesterol 1mg; Carbohydrate 70.7g; Sugars 10.9g; Protein 15.1g

CHAPTER EIGHT: STOCKS, SIDES AND SAUCES

SLOW COOKER CHICKEN STOCK

Preparation Time: 10 minutes
Cooking Time: 12 hours.
Serve: 4

Ingredients:

- 1 chicken carcass
- 2 stalks celery, cut in half
- 1 carrot, peeled, cut in half
- 1 medium onion, quartered
- 4 cloves garlic, smashed
- 1 handful parsley, sliced
- 4 sprigs fresh thyme
- 1 bay leaf
- ½ tablespoon black peppercorns
- 6 cups water

Directions:

1. Break the chicken carcass into pieces and place them into the slow cooker.
2. Add peppercorns, water and rest of the ingredients.
3. Cover this mixture with the lid and cook for 12 hours on LOW heat.
4. Strain the chicken stock through a fine sieve.
5. Serve.

Nutritional Value (Amount per Serving):

Calories 78; Fat 1.2g; Cholesterol 27mg; Carbohydrate 5.8g; Sugars 2.1g; Protein 10.9g

SLOW COOKER BONE BROTH

Preparation Time: 10 minutes
Cooking Time: 12 hours.
Serve: 8

Ingredients:
- 1 pound bones beef
- 2 cups celery stalks halved
- 1 cup carrots, halved
- 1 cup onion, quartered
- 2 sprigs fresh thyme
- 2 sprigs rosemary
- Salt and black pepper to taste
- 8 cups water

Directions:
1. Add onion, bones, water and rest of the ingredients to a slow cooker.
2. Cover this mixture with the lid and cook for 12 hours on LOW heat.
3. Strain the bone broth through a fine sieve.
4. Serve.

Nutritional Value (Amount per Serving):
Calories 90; Fat 2.2g; Cholesterol 11mg; Carbohydrate 11.8g; Sugars 1.3g; Protein 7.7g

SLOW COOKER SPAGHETTI SAUCE

Preparation Time: 10 minutes
Cooking Time: 8 hours.
Serve: 8

Ingredients:

* 1 pound ground beef
* 1 tablespoon olive oil
* 28 ounces can crushed tomatoes
* 28 ounces diced tomatoes
* 6 ounces can tomato paste
* 2 tablespoons brown sugar
* 1/2 cup white onion, diced
* 2 garlic cloves, minced
* 1 tablespoon dried oregano
* 2 teaspoon dried basil
* 1 teaspoon salt
* ¼ teaspoon black pepper
* 1 pinch red pepper flakes

Directions:

1. Sauté beef with oil in a skillet until brown then transfer to a slow cooker.
2. Stir in tomatoes and rest of the ingredients.
3. Cover this sauce with the lid and cook for 8 hours on LOW heat.
4. Mix well and serve warm.

Nutritional Value (Amount per Serving):

Calories 250; Fat 4.7g; Cholesterol 51mg; Carbohydrate 33.4g; Sugars 5.5g; Protein 24.1g

SLOW COOKER TOMATO SAUCE

Preparation Time: 10 minutes
Cooking Time: 7 hours.
Serve: 8

Ingredients:
* 3 x 14 ounces tins tomatoes, chopped
* 1 onion, chopped
* 5 garlic cloves, minced
* 2 tablespoons tomato puree
* 1 teaspoon dried thyme
* 2 sprigs fresh basil, chopped
* Salt, to taste
* Black pepper, to taste

Directions:
1. Add tomatoes, onion, basil and rest of the ingredients to the slow cooker.
2. Cover this sauce with the lid and cook for 7 hours on HIGH heat.
3. Blend this sauce in a blender until smooth.
4. Serve.

Nutritional Value (Amount per Serving):
Calories 39; Fat 0.1g; Cholesterol 0mg; Carbohydrate 8.4g; Sugars 3.9g; Protein 1.4g

CARAMELIZED ONIONS

Preparation Time: 10 minutes
Cooking Time: 10 hours.
Serve: 16

Ingredients:

* ¼ cup melted butter
* 8 onions, thinly sliced
* 1 teaspoon salt

Directions:

1. Add onions, butter and salt to a slow cooker.
2. Cover these onions with the lid and cook for 10 hours on LOW heat.
3. Serve.

Nutritional Value (Amount per Serving):

Calories 95; Fat 5.9g; Cholesterol 15mg; Carbohydrate 10.3g; Sugars 4.7g; Protein 1.3g

SPICED APPLESAUCE

Preparation Time: 10 minutes
Cooking Time: 8 ½ hours.
Serve: 8

Ingredients:

* 8 apples, peeled, cored, and sliced
* ½ cup water
* ¾ cup packed brown sugar
* ½ teaspoon pumpkin pie spice

Directions:

1. Add apples, and water to the slow cooker.
2. Cover this mixture with the lid and cook for 8 hours on LOW heat.
3. Stir in pumpkin pie spices and brown sugar.
4. Cover again and continue cooking for 30 minutes at LOW heat.
5. Mix well and serve.

Nutritional Value (Amount per Serving):

Calories 168; Fat 0.4g; Cholesterol 0mg; Carbohydrate 44.2g; Sugars 36.4g; Protein 0.6gg

CHAPTER NINE: DESSERT

CHOCOLATE CARAMEL CAKE

Preparation Time: 10 minutes
Cooking Time: 3 hours.
Serve: 8

Ingredients:

* 1½ cup all-purpose flour
* ¾ cup granulated sugar
* ⅓ cup unsweetened cocoa powder
* 1½ teaspoons baking powder
* ¾ teaspoon salt
* 1 cup milk
* ⅔ cup vegetable oil
* 1½ teaspoons vanilla extract
* 1½ cups semi-sweet chocolate chips
* 1 cup milk chocolate chips
* 1 can Dulce De Leche
* ⅓ cup heavy cream

Directions:

1. Grease 4-quart slow cooker with non-stick cooking spray.
2. Mix flour with salt, baking powder, cocoa powder, and sugar in a mixing bowl.
3. Stir in vanilla extract, oil and milk then mix until smooth.
4. Fold in chocolate chips and spread this chocolate chip batter in the slow cooker.
5. Add heavy cream and Dulce De Leche to a microwave safe bowl.
6. Heat this dulce de leche for 45 seconds in the microwave.
7. Mix well then spread this creamy mixture over the cake batter in the slow cooker.
8. Cover this cake batter with the lid and cook for 3 hours on HIGH heat.
9. Slice and serve.

Nutritional Value (Amount per Serving):

Calories 351; Fat 13.2g; Cholesterol 5mg; Carbohydrate 53.2g; Sugars 12.8g; Protein 6.2g

BLACKBERRY COBBLER

Preparation Time: 10 minutes
Cooking Time: 2 ½ hours.
Serve: 8

Ingredients:

Blackberry layer
* 5 cups blackberries, rinsed and drained
* 1 tablespoon cornstarch
* 2 tablespoons butter melted
* ¼ cup sugar

Topping
* 1 tablespoon sugar
* ¼ teaspoon cinnamon

Cobbler layer
* 1 ¼ cup all-purpose flour
* ¾ cup sugar
* 1 ½ teaspoon baking powder
* ½ teaspoon salt
* 1 cup milk
* 1 teaspoon vanilla extract
* 2 tablespoons salted butter melted

Directions:

1. Add blackberries, 2 tablespoons butter, 1 tablespoon cornstarch and ¼ cup sugar to the slow cooker.
2. Toss well and lightly mash the berries with a potato masher.
3. Mix flour with sugar, salt and rest of the cobbler layer ingredients in a bowl.
4. Spread this cobbler mixture over the blackberries.
5. Mix cinnamon with sugar in a bowl for topping.
6. Drizzle this sugar over the cobbler layer.
7. Cover this cobbler with the lid and cook for 2 ½ hours at HIGH heat.
8. Serve with ice cream.

Nutritional Value (Amount per Serving):

Calories 230; Fat 4.4g; Cholesterol 12mg; Carbohydrate 43.7g; Sugars 16.2g; Protein 5.7g

PEANUT BUTTER CHOCOLATE CHIP BLONDIES

Preparation Time: 10 minutes
Cooking Time: 1 ½ hours.
Serve: 8

Ingredients:

* ½ cup 1 tablespoon all-purpose flour
* ¼ teaspoon baking powder
* ¼ cup sugar
* 3 tablespoons packed light brown sugar
* 2 tablespoons butter
* 2 tablespoons creamy peanut butter
* 1 large egg
* 1 teaspoon vanilla
* ⅔ cup mini chocolate chips

Directions:

1. Grease a 3 ½ quart slow cooker with cooking spray.
2. Beat butter, sugar, peanut butter and brown sugar in a bowl with an electric mixer.
3. Add egg and vanilla then beat until smooth.
4. Stir in dry flour and baking powder then mix again until lump-free.
5. Fold in chocolate chips and mix evenly.
6. Spread this chocolate chip blondie batter in the slow cooker.
7. Cover this batter with the lid and cook for 1 ½ hours on HIGH heat.
8. Allow the blondies to cool and slice into 12 pieces.

Nutritional Value (Amount per Serving):

Calories 178; Fat 9.7g; Cholesterol 34mg; Carbohydrate 20.4g; Sugars 17.4g ; Protein 3.1g

S'MORES CAKE

Preparation Time: 10 minutes
Cooking Time: 4 hours.
Serve: 8

Ingredients:

- 1 (15.25 ounces) box chocolate cake mix
- 3 large eggs
- 1 cup sour cream
- 1 cup water
- 1 cup all-purpose flour
- 3/4 cup granulated sugar
- 2 cups marshmallows, cut into 4 slices
- 1 jar marshmallow creme
- 3/4 cup chocolate chips
- 4 whole graham crackers, broken

Directions:

1. Grease the slow cooker's pot with cooking spray.
2. Beat eggs with sour cream and water in a bowl.
3. Stir in sugar and flour then mix well until smooth.
4. Fold in 1 cup of marshmallows then mix well.
5. Spread this mixture in the slow cooker, cover it with the lid and cook for 4 hours on LOW heat.
6. Add marshmallow cream to a bowl and heat in the microwave for 20 seconds.
7. Spread the marshmallow cream over the cooked cake.
8. Add graham crackers, marshmallows and chocolate chips on top.
9. Slice and serve with ice cream.

Nutritional Value (Amount per Serving):

Calories 260; Fat 8.2g; Cholesterol 82mg; Carbohydrate 42.9g; Sugars 25g; Protein 5.2g

PEACH COBBLER

Preparation Time: 10 minutes
Cooking Time: 4 hours.
Serve: 8

Ingredients:

- 8 medium ripe peaches, sliced
- 1 1/4 cups granulated sugar
- 3/4 cup whole wheat flour
- 1/2 cup all-purpose flour
- 2 teaspoons baking powder
- 1/2 teaspoon baking soda
- 1/4 teaspoon salt
- 1/2 cup unsalted butter, sliced
- Vanilla ice cream, to serve

Directions:

10. Add peaches to a pan filled with boiling water and cook for a minute.
11. Drain and transfer the peaches to a bowl, placed in an ice bath.
12. Peel the peaches and slice them.
13. Spread the peaches in a slow cooker and drizzle ¼ cup sugar on top.
14. Mix flours with salt, baking soda, baking powder and remaining 1 cup sugar in a bowl.
15. Spread this mixture over the peaches and place the butter slices on top.
16. Cover the cobbler with the lid and cook for 4 hours on LOW heat.
17. Serve with ice cream on top.

Nutritional Value (Amount per Serving):

Calories 344; Fat 12.2g; Cholesterol 31mg; Carbohydrate 59.1g; Sugars 45.7g; Protein 3.8g

CONCLUSION

So if you are tired of traditional slow cooking and want to make it easier for yourself then, it's about time that you buy a suitable slow cooker and use it as an efficient, single-unit cooking appliance. Now you can leave everything on the machine, and it will cook flavorsome meals without your active supervision. You can leave your food for hours in the slow cooker, and it will maintain the temperature and the cooking time on its own. All you need to do is to set the time and temperature. Every slow cooker comes with low to med to high temperatures settings which can be used for hours. In this cookbook, you have all the delicious and basic slow cooking recipes that you can cook using any slow cooker. Try them at home, add them to your menu and spread the magic of heartwarming flavors and aromas.

CPSIA information can be obtained
at www.ICGtesting.com
Printed in the USA
BVHW051154201221
624506BV00009B/982